I Get It from My Mother!

by Mrs. Kishbaugh's Class
with Tony Stead

capstone

What do your parents give you? Parents give you love, food, and a home. They also gave you your eye, hair, and skin color, and even your body shape. These things come from your genes. Plants and animals have genes, too. But what are genes? How do genes work?

What Are Genes?

by Avery, Ayden, Jeremie, Jordan, and Lex

Have you ever wondered why you look like someone in your family? A girl may have blue eyes like her mother or maybe brown hair like her father. This is because of genes. So what are genes anyway?

Genes are tiny structures inside your cells. They are very powerful, but you cannot see them because they are so tiny. Humans have thousands of genes.

GENES
MAKE
US DIFFERENT!!!

Genes are carried in molecules called DNA. Long strands of DNA make up chromosomes. Every human being has 23 pairs of chromosomes. One of these pairs decides whether you are a girl or a boy.

What Do Genes Do?

Genes are like instructions for your body. These instructions come partly from your parents. They give you the color of your eyes, hair, and skin. Have you ever wondered why identical twins look alike? It's because of their genes! Genes make you who you are. Every living thing has genes, but everyone is different.

Genes Are Passed to Offspring

by Ali, Allison, Kierra, Maia, and Maurice

Did you know that genes are passed to you from your parents? Genes are what make you look like you. For example, you might have blue eyes or brown hair. Your genes help give you these traits, or features.

Traits

Traits are also called characteristics. Every trait has two genes. One gene is from your dad, and the other gene is from your mom.

A trait can be a behavior or what you look like. Inherited and acquired traits are the two different types of traits.

this is the mom
this is the baby

Inherited and Acquired Traits

Some traits come from genes passed from parents to their children. These are inherited traits. For example, you can have blue eyes from your dad and brown hair from your mom.

Acquired traits come from your environment or your experiences. The word "acquire" means to get something. For example, if you get a scar on your knee, it is an acquired trait because you weren't born with it. You got it from an experience in your life.

Both inherited and acquired traits are important. If you didn't have traits, you wouldn't be yourself!

I Look Like my mom because of Genes.

my Brother got his blue eyes from my Dad.

Dominant and Recessive Genes

by Christian, Gabe, Lasse, Matthew, and Megan

Did you know that if both your mom and dad have brown hair, it doesn't mean that you will, too? You could get a recessive hair color gene and your hair could be blond. For example, it could have been passed down from your grandparents or ancestors.

Mendel's Pea Plant Experiment

Gregor Mendel was a man of science who lived in the 1800s. Mendel wanted to see what would happen if he grew a new pea plant from a short pea plant and a tall pea plant. Mendel thought the new pea plant would be medium height. But he got a tall pea plant instead. Because of his experiment, we learned that tall pea plants are dominant and short pea plants are recessive.

Dominant Genes

Dominant genes are powerful. When dominant genes are passed to a child, they control the way the child looks. The child will have the traits of the parent that passed on the dominant genes. Examples of dominant genes are brown eyes.

Recessive Genes

Recessive genes are super weak and are not as powerful as dominant genes. Recessive genes get passed to children the same way as dominant genes. But you need two recessive genes to get a recessive trait.

It is important to know how dominant and recessive genes work. By knowing about dominant and recessive genes, you know what makes you one of a kind. When you first learn about dominant and recessive genes, you may be confused. But genes can help you learn why you have certain traits and not others.

Probability

by Dallas, JT, Katelyn, Kaylee, and Noah

Do you know why you look like your parents? It's because you get 50 percent of your genes from your mom and 50 percent from your dad. Do you know what probability is? Probability is the chance that each of your traits will come from your mom or your dad.

Where Did I Get That From?

Even though you got half your genes from your mom and half from your dad, sometimes you can't see certain traits. That's because they come from recessive genes. If your mom has brown eyes and your dad has blue eyes, you could use a gene probability chart to help find where a trait came from. Brothers and sisters might even have different hair and eye colors.

Gene Probability Chart

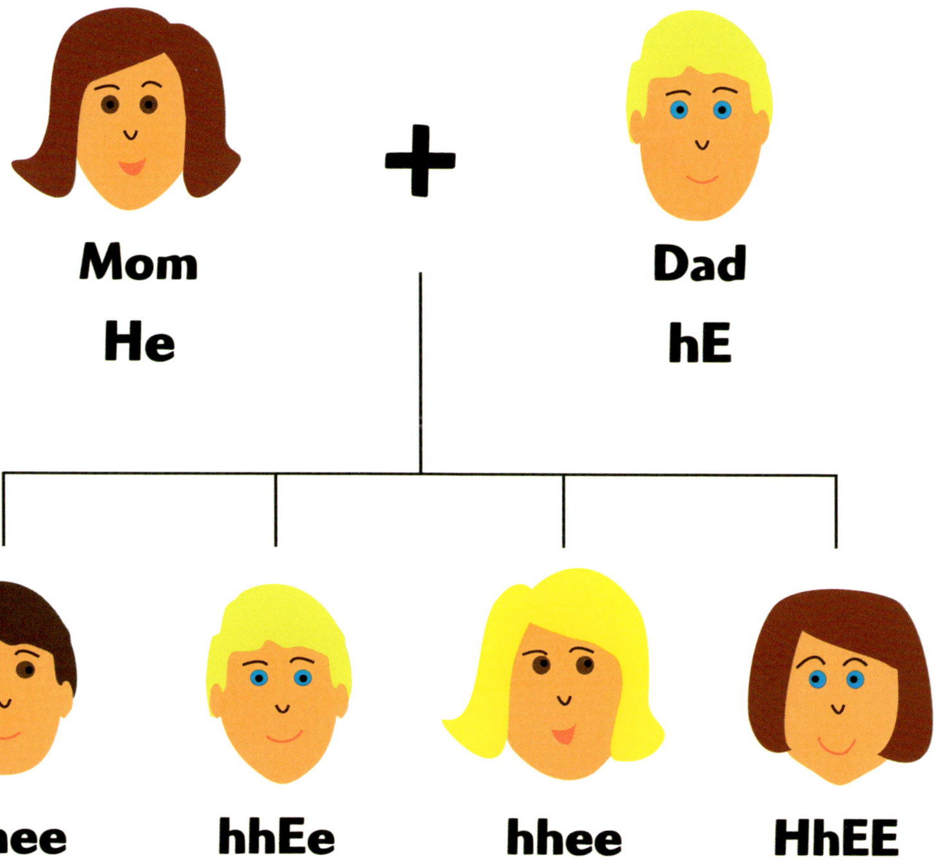

Punnett Squares

A Punnett Square can help you figure out the odds of parents passing on particular genes to their children. A Punnett Square can help you figure out what color eyes their children will have if the mother has brown eyes and the father has blue eyes.

Punnett Square

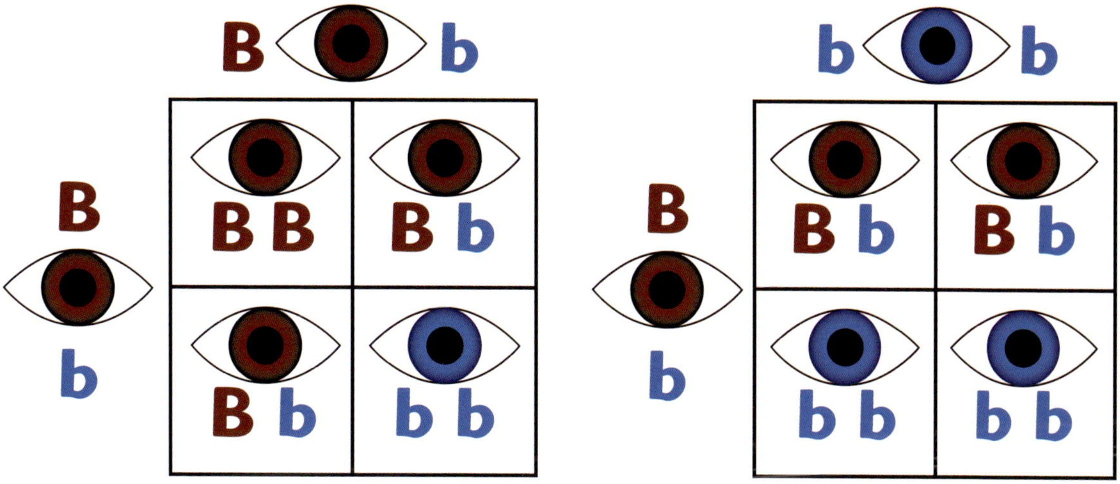

B - dominant brown eye gene
b - recessive blue eye gene

BB brown eyes
Bb brown eyes
bb blue eyes

Brown eyes are dominant. If one parent has brown eyes and one has blue eyes, the only way their child will have blue eyes is if the child gets two blue eye genes.

Mutations

by Andy, Eliza, Ian, and Riley

Have you heard of a two-headed turtle or seen a person with 12 toes? Sounds strange, right? These differences are caused by DNA mutations. Mutations can happen for many reasons, like when there is one more or one less gene in a person's DNA.

What Are Mutations?

Mutations are inside the cells and cause cells to divide incorrectly. Researchers have found more than 4,000 diseases caused by mutations. Mutations are in every living thing, but most of the time, you don't even know they're there. But they may cause you to grow differently.

Ears
This is a cat that has
a mutation that caused
it to have four ears.

What Can Mutations Do?

Mutations can happen if an organism is exposed to harmful chemicals when it is forming. The chemicals can damage the organism's DNA and cause mutations. Some mutations are harmless, but some cause disease or other conditions. For example, as a result of a mutation, a starfish might grow only four arms instead of five.

Another example of a mutation is a cat named Venus. One side of her face has a green eye and black fur and the other side has a blue eye and yellow fur. This happened because of a mutation in the her DNA. Having two different colored eyes can also happen in humans, dogs, and other animals.

Everyone has mutations inside their cells, but most of them do not cause diseases or other conditions. You have mutations inside you right now! You just don't know it!

You've learned a lot about genes, the building blocks of life. Suppose you are describing your nose and you say, "I got it from my mother!" A friend asks, "What do you mean?" How do you answer?

illustrated by Katelyn